The Great Getaway

STUNT BUNNY

TAMSYN MURRAY
ILLUSTRATED BY LEE WILDISH

Published by Pearson Education Limited, Edinburgh Gate, Harlow, Essex, CM20 2JE
Registered company number: 872828

www.pearsonschools.co.uk

Text originally published by Simon & Schuster Children's Books in 2010 as part of *Stunt Bunny: Showbiz Sensation*.

Text © Tamsyn Murray 2010
Cover and inside illustrations © 2010 Lee Wildish
Cover design by Bigtop

Interior illustrations and text all used by kind permission from Simon & Schuster Children's Books.

The right of Tamsyn Murray and Lee Wildish to be identified as the author and illustrator of this work respectively has been asserted by them in accordance with sections 77 and 78 of the Copyright, Designs and Patents Act, 1988.

First published 2012

16 15 14 13
10 9 8 7 6 5 4 3

British Library Cataloguing in Publication Data
A catalogue record for this book is available from the British Library

ISBN 978 0 435 07637 5

Copyright notice
All rights reserved. No part of this publication may be reproduced in any form or by any means (including photocopying or storing it in any medium by electronic means and whether or not transiently or incidentally to some other use of this publication) without the written permission of the copyright owner, except in accordance with the provisions of the Copyright, Designs and Patents Act 1988 or under the terms of a licence issued by the Copyright Licensing Agency, Saffron House, 6–10 Kirby Street, London EC1N 8TS (www.cla.co.uk). Applications for the copyright owner's written permission should be addressed to the publisher.

Printed and bound in Malaysia (CTP-VP)

Acknowledgements
We would like to thank the children and teachers of Bangor Central Integrated Primary School, NI; Barley Hill School, Thame; Bishop Henderson C of E Primary School, Somerset; Brookside Community Primary School, Somerset; Catcott Primary School, Somerset; Cheddington Combined School, Buckinghamshire; Cofton Primary School, Birmingham; Dair House Independent School, Buckinghamshire; Deal Parochial School, Kent; Lawthorn Primary School, North Ayrshire; Newbold Riverside Primary School, Rugby and Windmill Primary School, Oxford for their invaluable help in the development and trialling of the Bug Club resources.

Every effort has been made to contact copyright holders of material reproduced in this book. Any omissions will be rectified in subsequent printings if notice is given to the publisher.

Contents

Chapter 1
An Unexpected Visitor......4

Chapter 2
The Magician Returns......16

Chapter 3
Trusty Teeth to the Rescue!......23

Chapter 1
An Unexpected Visitor

It's not easy being a Stunt Bunny. If I'm not meeting my adoring fans, then I'm rehearsing my latest dare-devil trick.

You see, I'm the star of *Superpets*, the Saturday night TV show where animals take to the stage.

Some people think my life is all chomping on carrots and waggling my powder-puff tail but there's a lot more to it than that. Trust me, being *this* cute is hard work. Luckily my owner, Susie Wilson, is pretty clever for an eight-year-old. She understands exactly what a celebrity pet needs.

When the doorbell rang early one Saturday morning, I didn't pay much attention at first. It was probably another one of my fans begging for an autograph. They often came to the door wearing flashing, furry ears and t-shirts with my picture on.

So I was only half listening to the conversation which floated in from the front door.

"I, ze Great Maldini, need a rabbit for my world-famous magic show. I 'ave seen your 'Arriet on ze TV and she ees perfect for ze job."

My ears stood on end at the mention of my name. Another job? Surely working on *Superpets* was enough?

Susie's dad thought it over.

"We're busy enough taking Harriet to and from the TV studio, Mr Maldini. I don't think we can take on any more work."

"You don't understand, Signor Wilson. I want to buy your bunny. Name your price!"

I shuffled uneasily on my chair. I didn't want a new owner. Susie would be sad and I'd miss her and the rest of the Wilson family terribly.

Would Susie's dad know that, though?

"I'm afraid she's not for sale," he said firmly.

"Signor Wilson, everything ees for sale. 'Ow about five thousand pounds?"

There was a long silence. My heart pounded uncomfortably.

"That's a lot of money. It would pay for our holiday to Spain next month ..." I could almost hear Mr Wilson's brain whirring, "... but the answer is still no."

"Ten thousand!" The Great Maldini cried. "Twenty thousand pounds! I must 'ave zat rabbit!"

This time, Mr Wilson's voice had an edge of annoyance to it. "I'm sorry, Mr Maldini, you cannot buy Harriet."

"Zis ees not over," The Great Maldini said, sounding angry. "You 'ave not heard ze last of ze Great Maldini!"

There was a loud bang as the front door slammed shut. I heaved a sigh of relief and went back to munching my carrot.

"Who was that?" Susie's mum asked as Mr Wilson came into the kitchen.

"A famous magician, or so he said," Mr Wilson sniffed. "He wanted to buy Harriet to use in his show."

Mrs Wilson frowned. "You said no, didn't you? Harriet is part of the family now."

"Of course I did." Mr Wilson said. "I just hope he got the message."

So did I, but I had the strangest feeling we'd be seeing The Great Maldini again.

Chapter 2
The Magician Returns

I was looking forward to our family holiday. *Superpets* had finished filming for the summer break and a week in sunny Spain sounded like the perfect way to relax.

I could already picture myself on a beach, sunglasses on my nose and a cool drink in my paw.

So, imagine my disgust when I was left behind to be bunny-sat by Mrs Green from next door. Don't get me wrong, Mrs Green is very nice, but it hardly seemed fair that the rest of my family were off sunbathing while I was stuck in rainy old Britain.

I was very grumpy on the day Susie and the rest of the family were due home. Mrs Green was giving my hutch a clean before they arrived so I was locked up in an old cat basket. *Brrrring!* The sound of the doorbell made me prick up my ears. Mrs Green went to answer it.

A minute later, she was leading a tall, thin man through to the garden with a puzzled frown on her face.

"I don't remember the Wilsons mentioning you'd be coming," she said. "Are you sure Harriet needs to have her claws clipped?"

The man smiled. "Zey probably forgot in ze excitement of going on holiday, no?"

I twitched my nose, thinking hard. That voice was familiar; where had I heard it before? Also, what was that rubbish about my claws being clipped? The vet had only just done them. Something odd was going on.

"Well, I suppose you wouldn't be here otherwise."

Mrs Green lifted up my basket and passed it to the man.

He peered into through the bars, dark eyes glittering. "Come along, 'Arriet. Time for me to work my magic on you!"

My eyes went wide as I realised who he was. He was no claw-clipper. He was The Great Maldini and since Mr Wilson had refused to sell me, he was going to steal me away! Somehow, I had to warn Mrs Green. But how?

Chapter 3

Trusty Teeth to the Rescue!

I was in deep droppings. The Great Maldini was carrying me down the garden path and despite my frantic squeaking, Mrs Green hadn't realised that anything was wrong.

She waved The Great Maldini off as he strode towards a shiny, red sports car. Mrs Green was going to be no help at all.
I was on my own.

Suddenly I had an idea. With determination, I started chomping on the straps holding the basket door shut.

They were tough and hurt my teeth but I kept on gnawing.

Seconds ticked by. The Great Maldini reached into his pocket and pulled out his car keys.

Then I heard a familiar voice shout, "Harriet!" It was Susie.

I looked up to see her running along the pavement towards me, her face twisted in horror.

The Great Maldini saw Susie too. In a flash, he'd pushed the cat basket through the open window and onto the front seat of the sports car. He dashed around to the driver's side.

Time was running out. I chewed as though my life depended on it. Which it did, sort of.

Gnash, gnash! With a final bite of my trusty teeth, the last strap gave way. I pushed my nose against the basket door and wriggled through the gap.

The Great Maldini had started the engine. It *vroomed* into life with a great roar and the car started to roll along the road. I scrambled on top of the basket and gazed at Susie's tearful face through the open window.

"Harriet, come back!" she cried, running after the car.

The Great Maldini glanced over at me, grinning in triumph. "It ees too late, little rabbit. Even ze Stunt Bunny cannot escape zis time!"

It was now or never. I was about to perform the biggest stunt of my life. Closing my eyes, I leaped through the open window and cart-wheeled through the air.

One spin, two spins, three spins ... for one heart-stopping moment I thought I'd got it wrong.

Then I landed with a *thud* in Susie's arms.

She hugged me tightly. "Oh, Harriet! I thought I'd lost you."

Susie's dad arrived behind her and shook his fist at the vanishing car of The Great Maldini, yelling "I'm calling the police, you thief!"

My racing heart gradually slowed down as Susie carried me back into the house. I nuzzled my velvet nose against her neck, happy to see her and relieved to be safe. It had been close but, in the end, the Wilsons had timed the return from their holiday perfectly.

It seemed that my *Superpets* training had saved me too.

Like I said before, it's not easy being a Stunt Bunny – but someone has to do it!